Gross Body JOKES to Tickle Your FUNNY BONE

Linda Bozzo

Enslow Elementary

an imprint of

Enslow Publishers, Inc.

40 Industrial Road
Box 398
Berkeley Heights, NJ 07922
USA

http://www.enslow.com

Enslow Elementary, an imprint of Enslow Publishers, Inc.

Enslow Elementary® is a registered trademark of Enslow Publishers, Inc.

Library of Congress Cataloging-in-Publication Data

Bozzo, Linda.
   Gross body jokes to tickle your funny bone / Linda Bozzo.
       p. cm. — (Funny bone jokes)
   Includes bibliographical references and index.
   Summary: "Includes jokes, limericks, knock-knock jokes, tongue twisters, and fun facts about different muscles, organs, bones, and teeth, and describes how to write your own limerick"—Provided by publisher.
   ISBN 978-0-7660-3540-9
   1. Wit and humor, Juvenile. 2. Human body—Humor. I. Title.
PN6166.B69 2010
818'.602—dc22

                                2010004192

Printed in the United States of America

122010 Lake Book Manufacturing, Inc., Melrose Park, IL

10 9 8 7 6 5 4 3 2 1

To Our Readers: We have done our best to make sure all Internet Addresses in this book were active and appropriate when we went to press. However, the author and the publisher have no control over and assume no liability for the material available on those Internet sites or on other Web sites they may link to. Any comments or suggestions can be sent by e-mail to comments@enslow.com or to the address on the back cover.

♻ Enslow Publishers, Inc., is committed to printing our books on recycled paper. The paper in every book contains 10% to 30% post-consumer waste (PCW). The cover board on the outside of each book contains 100% PCW. Our goal is to do our part to help young people and the environment too!

Illustration Credits: © Clipart.com, a division of Getty Images, all clipart and photos except © Shutterstock, p. 4 (eyeball).

Cover Illustration: © Clipart.com, a division of Getty Images.

Contents

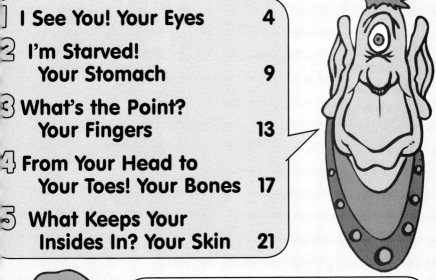

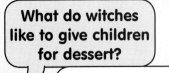

What do witches like to give children for dessert?

Eye scream!

FUN FACTS

IT'S TRUE.

What color eyes do you have? Are they green or are they maybe blue or brown? The color of the eye depends on the iris. Look in the mirror. The colored part of your eye is called the iris. The iris controls the amount of light that enters the eye. Light enters through the pupil, or the small opening in the center of the iris. The pupil gets smaller with more light and bigger when there is less light.

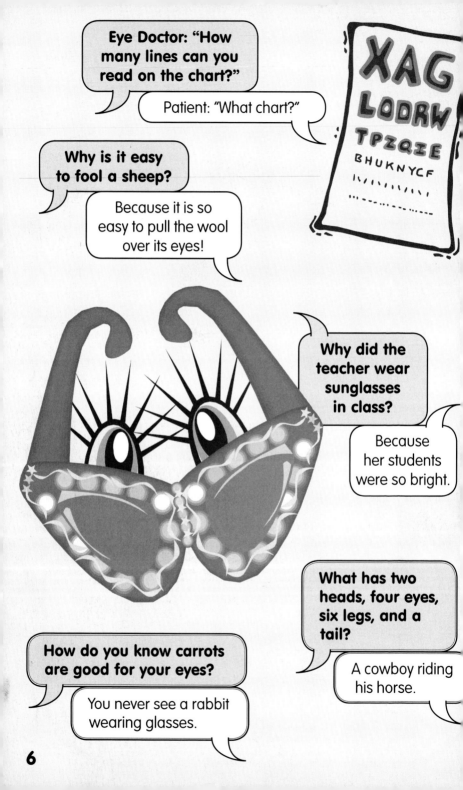

Eye Doctor: "How many lines can you read on the chart?"

Patient: "What chart?"

Why is it easy to fool a sheep?

Because it is so easy to pull the wool over its eyes!

Why did the teacher wear sunglasses in class?

Because her students were so bright.

What has two heads, four eyes, six legs, and a tail?

A cowboy riding his horse.

How do you know carrots are good for your eyes?

You never see a rabbit wearing glasses.

What did one eye say to the other eye?

Between you and me, something smells.

Knock, Knock!

Who's there?

Iris.

Iris who?

Iris you would open the door.

Each time you see this squiggly box, it is a tongue twister! Try saying it five times fast!

Sally sees six sleepy sheep when Sally should be sleeping.

What do you call a lion with no eyes?

Lon!

What can travel all over the world without anyone seeing it?

The wind.

It's curious how curious I am. I eyeball everything. I am what I sound like. I am. I am. I am! What am I?

An eye.

Knock, Knock!

Who's there?

Don.

Don who?

Don be afraid…look into my eyes…you are feeling sleepy…

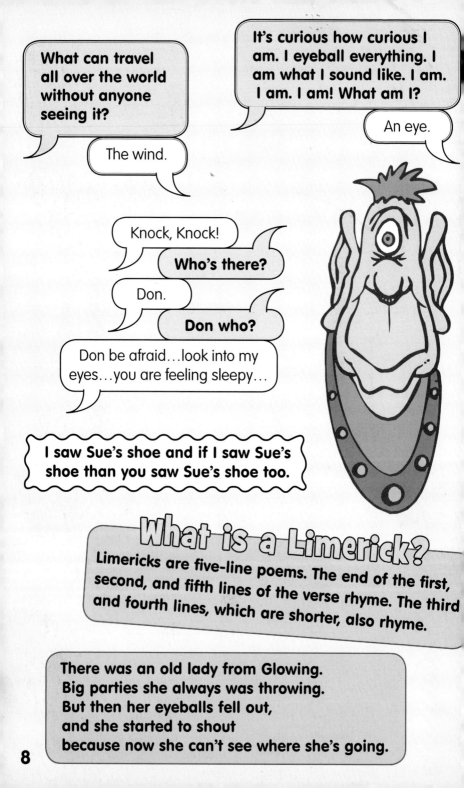

I saw Sue's shoe and if I saw Sue's shoe than you saw Sue's shoe too.

What is a Limerick?

Limericks are five-line poems. The end of the first, second, and fifth lines of the verse rhyme. The third and fourth lines, which are shorter, also rhyme.

There was an old lady from Glowing.
Big parties she always was throwing.
But then her eyeballs fell out,
and she started to shout
because now she can't see where she's going.

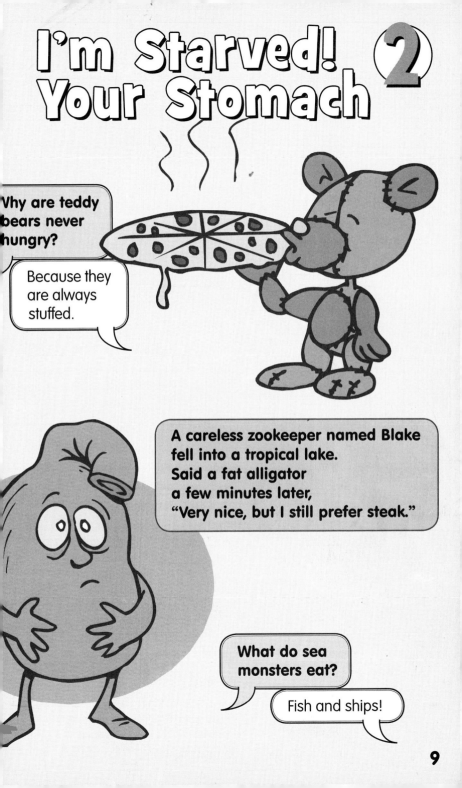

I'm Starved!
Your Stomach

Why are teddy bears never hungry?

Because they are always stuffed.

A careless zookeeper named Blake
fell into a tropical lake.
Said a fat alligator
a few minutes later,
"Very nice, but I still prefer steak."

What do sea monsters eat?

Fish and ships!

FUN FACTS

Are you ever sitting in class and everything is quiet? All of a sudden your stomach makes a soft growling sound. Stomach growling can happen at any time. Ever wonder why your stomach growls? Growling can happen because you are hungry. It can also happen after you eat. Your food takes many twists and turns through your body. Along the way, pockets of air and gas form. These pockets make the growling noise in your stomach and intestines.

IT'S TRUE.

Knock, Knock!

Who's there?

U-8.

U-8 who?

U-8 my candy bar!

What kind of button can't you unbutton?

A belly button.

There was young lady of Spain
who was dreadfully sick on a train,
not once, but again,
and again and again
and again and again and again.

Shelly's stomach shook on the ship, so Shelly got sick.

Knock, Knock!

Who's there?

Justin.

Justin who?

Justin time for dinner!

Knock, Knock!

Who's there?

Gladys.

Gladys who?

Gladys lunch time, I'm starved!

The silly sound from Sammy's sister's son's spoiled stomach sounded somewhat serious.

What do you call a monkey with no fingers?

A monkey.

Knock, Knock!

Who's there?

Raisin.

Raisin who?

Raisin our hands before we speak.

How many pens could a hen hold if a hen had hands to hold pens?

Why didn't the finger cross the road?

There was no point.

14

FUN FACTS

Think of all the things you do using your fingers. Each of your hands has twenty-eight muscles. That is a total of fifty-six muscles in both hands. But do you know what parts of your hands do not have any muscles? Would it surprise you to know that it is your fingers? There are no muscles inside the fingers. The muscles that control the fingers are in the palm and forearm. What's the point? Next time you tie your shoes or write with your pencil notice how important your fingers are.

IT'S TRUE.

If you're pointing at me I suppose
it should only be done with your toes.
But pointing is rude
except at your food.
It's a rule that everyone knows.

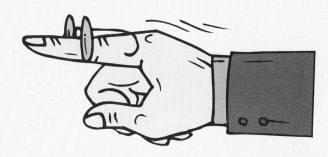

There was an old lady from Bands
who had the most beautiful hands.
But when her fingers got cold,
she became very bold
and of course made a quick change of plans.

Knock, Knock!

Who's there?

Hurda.

Hurda who?

Hurda my finger
in the door!

Five fingers fling four fleas five times.

From Your Head to Your Toes! Your Bones

4

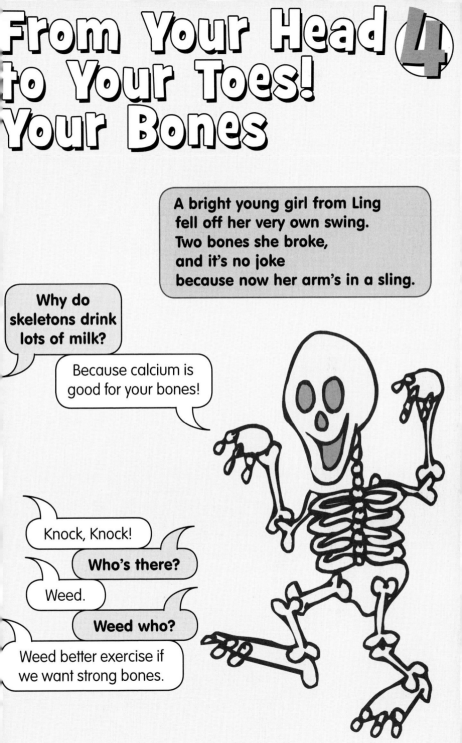

A bright young girl from Ling
fell off her very own swing.
Two bones she broke,
and it's no joke
because now her arm's in a sling.

Why do skeletons drink lots of milk?

Because calcium is good for your bones!

Knock, Knock!

Who's there?

Weed.

Weed who?

Weed better exercise if we want strong bones.

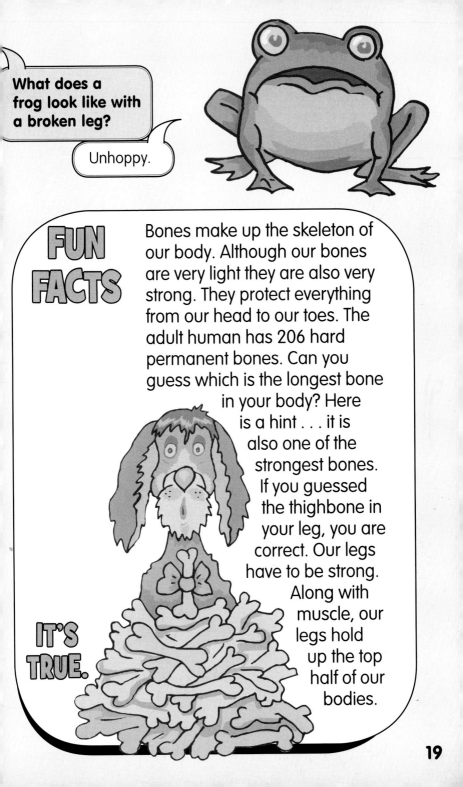

What does a frog look like with a broken leg?

Unhoppy.

FUN FACTS

Bones make up the skeleton of our body. Although our bones are very light they are also very strong. They protect everything from our head to our toes. The adult human has 206 hard permanent bones. Can you guess which is the longest bone in your body? Here is a hint . . . it is also one of the strongest bones. If you guessed the thighbone in your leg, you are correct. Our legs have to be strong. Along with muscle, our legs hold up the top half of our bodies.

IT'S TRUE.

What Keeps Your Insides In? Your Skin

5

What's a mosquito's favorite sport?

Skin diving.

There was a fellow named Mike,
who liked to ride on his bike.
Then he hit a tree,
and skinned his knee.
That was the end of Mike's bike.

Knock, Knock!

Who's there?

Snow use.

Snow use who?

Snow use, I'm already sweating!

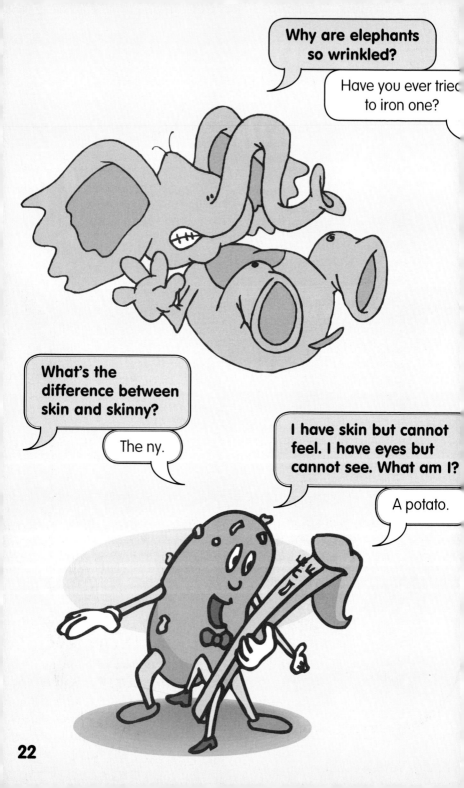

What did one banana say to the other banana?

I love the skin I'm in.

There are many different organs in your body, such as your liver and your heart. But do you know which is the largest organ in your body? You might be surprised to learn it is your skin. That's right. Your skin covers your entire body. The skin of an average adult weighs around six pounds. That is twice as much as a brain! You might wonder how that is possible when you shed skin cells every minute of every day. New skins cells are always replacing the old ones. During your lifetime, it is possible that you will shed more than forty pounds of your skin.

IT'S TRUE.

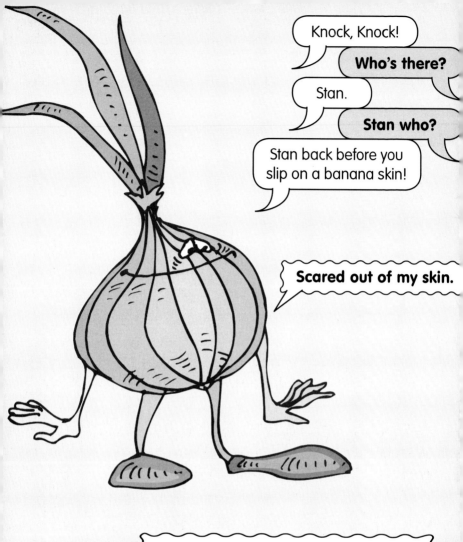

Snake's smooth skin keeps snake safe.

There was a big snake at the zoo,
whose skin was the color of blue.
When he came out,
the children would shout,
"We want to be blue like you!"

Smile! Your Teeth

6

What has teeth but never goes to the dentist?

A comb!

What four letters does the dentist say to her patient?

ICDK (I see decay)

How did the dentist get across the river?

With a tooth ferry.

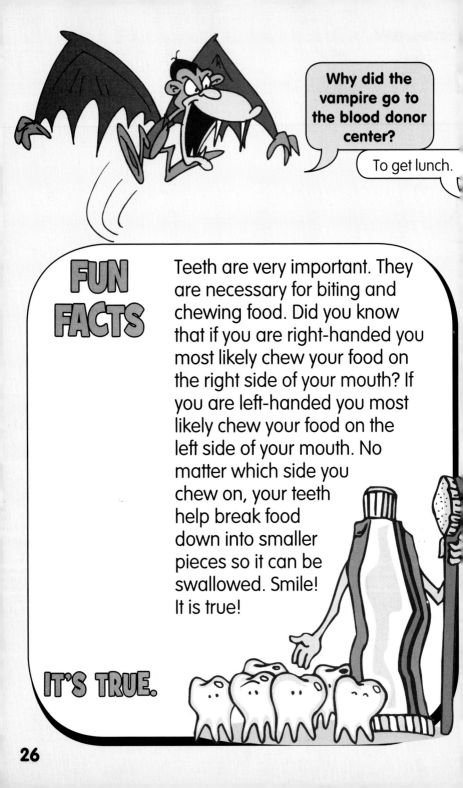

Why did the vampire go to the blood donor center?

To get lunch.

FUN FACTS

Teeth are very important. They are necessary for biting and chewing food. Did you know that if you are right-handed you most likely chew your food on the right side of your mouth? If you are left-handed you most likely chew your food on the left side of your mouth. No matter which side you chew on, your teeth help break food down into smaller pieces so it can be swallowed. Smile! It is true!

IT'S TRUE.

What do you call a dentist in the army?

A drill sergeant!

Why did the piecrust go to the dentist?

It needed a filling!

There was a young fellow called Hugh
who went to a neighboring zoo.
The lion opened wide
and said, "Come inside,
and bring all the family too."

Knock, Knock!

Who's there?

Tuba.

Tuba who?

Tuba toothpaste

An elderly man called Keith
mislaid his false set of teeth.
They'd been laid on a chair,
he'd forgot they were there,
sat down and was bitten beneath!

If Stu chews shoes, should Stu choose
the shoes he chews?

What is the best thing
to put in a sandwich?

Your teeth!

Knock, Knock!

Who's there?

Will you.

Will you who?

Will you be my Valentine?

What do you call a doctor with a bright green stethoscope?

Doctor!

I am a man without blood or a heart. Who am I?

A snowman.

Harvey the hairy hedgehog has a heavy heart.

"Doctor, I'm here for my heart."

"Sorry, I don't have it!"

Knock, Knock!

Who's there?

Chest.

Chest who?

Chest my heart beating.

30

Your heart is an organ that is found in the center of your chest. It pumps blood throughout your body. The heart works by itself. It does not need your help. You got to love it! The size of a person's heart may be different but all hearts have a right half and left half. The wall that divides the right and left sides of the heart is the septum. Did you know that the two halves are completely different? They do not mix blood between them.

There was an old fellow named Pete,
and a young lady he wanted to meet.
But when he said, "Hi,"
he thought he might die.
In his feet he felt his heart beat.

What pilot loved
to the fly the most?

Amelia "Air-Heart."

How can you make
a heart hear?

Remove the *t*.

There once was a boy who ate
the vegetables off his plate.
They were good for his heart,
but before he could start,
he always shared with his date.

Move It or Lose It! Your Muscles

8

There once was a man named Kong
who thought he was really strong.
He tried to pick up
a little teacup,
and it took him longer than long.

Knock, Knock!

Who's there?

Carrie

Carrie who?

Carrie these boxes, they're not heavy!

What are the strongest days?

Saturday and Sunday. All the rest are weak days!

What does a moose get when he lifts weights?

Moosles.

What kind of animal can jump higher than the Empire State Building?

Any animal. The Empire State Building can't jump!

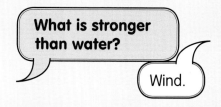

What is stronger than water?

Wind.

Move when you groove and you might lose shoes.

FUN FACTS

Did you know that you have more than thirty muscles just in your face? These are the muscles that help you smile when you are happy. They also help you frown when you are sad. Think those are busy muscles? Blink again! The busiest muscles in the body are the eye muscles. Scientists believe they move more than 100,000 times a day!

IT'S TRUE.

When is the best time to long-jump?

In a leap year.

What animal is the strongest?

A snail. He carries his house.

How many loads of laundry could lazy Linda lift if lazy Linda wasn't lazy?

There once was a man named Russell
who once had lots of muscle.
But he stopped working out
day in and day out,
and that was the end of his muscle.

Think About It! Your Brain

9

Your brain is an organ inside your head. It not only tells your body what to do, it tells you what to think and how to feel. Did you remember the answer on your test? Think about it. That is your brain at work. Are you feeling happy that you have the day off from school? That is a message from your brain, too. The brain is made up of about 80 percent water. Your brain also contains brain cells that are the longest living cells in the body. They can live an entire lifetime!

IT'S TRUE.

39

Knock, Knock!

Who's there?

Wilma.

Wilma who?

Wilma headache ever go away?

Which football player wears the biggest helmet?

The one with the biggest head.

Better brains are better than bigger brains.

There was an old man who said, "Gee!
I can't multiply seven by three!
Though fourteen seems plenty,
it might come to twenty,
I haven't the slightest idee!"

Smart students study smartly.

There was an old man who said, "Do tell me how I should add two and two? I think more and more that it makes about four, but I fear that is almost too few."

What do you call a hat for a brain?

A thinking cap.

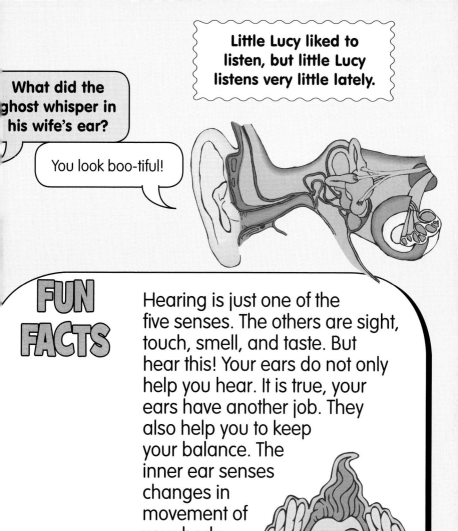

Little Lucy liked to listen, but little Lucy listens very little lately.

What did the ghost whisper in his wife's ear?

You look boo-tiful!

FUN FACTS

IT'S TRUE.

Hearing is just one of the five senses. The others are sight, touch, smell, and taste. But hear this! Your ears do not only help you hear. It is true, your ears have another job. They also help you to keep your balance. The inner ear senses changes in movement of your body. Therefore, it is the inner ear that allows us to move without falling.

LISTEN

What is the only thing you can break when you say its name?

Silence.

Knock, Knock!

Who's there?

Shirley.

Shirley who?

Shirley you know the sound of my voice by now.

There once was a lady named Wood,
who would sing whenever she could.
But people covered their ears
and filled up with tears
because she really wasn't that good.

If an ear can hear can hair breathe air?

Fun Activity

How to Write a Fun Limerick

A limerick is a funny, rhyming poem that is usually five lines. It's easy to write a limerick of your own.

First, brainstorm some rhyming words. Write them down on a piece of paper. Example: France, dance, pants, ants, true, knew, too, blue.

Next, number lines on a piece of paper from 1-5.

Write lines 1 and 2 so the last word in each line rhyme with each other.

Example:

1. There once was a man from France.

2. His friends thought he liked to dance.

Then write lines 3 and 4 so the last word in each line rhyme with each other.

Example:

3. But that was not true

4. And what no one knew

Finally, write line 5 so the last word rhymes with lines 1 and 2.

Example:

5. Was he really had ants in his pants.

Limericks are fun to write on your own or with a group of people.

Read More

Books

Chmielewski, Gary. *The Medical Zone: Jokes, Riddles, Tongue Twisters, and "Daffynitions."* Chicago, Ill.: Norwood House Press, 2009.

Phillips, Bob. *Awesome Knock Knock Jokes for Kids.* Eugene, Ore.: Harvest House Publishers, 2006.

Thomas, Lyn. *Jokes Ha! Ha! Ha! And Much More: The Ultimate Round-up of Jokes, Riddles, Facts, and Puzzles.* Toronto: Maple Tree Press, 2008.

Weitzman, Ilana, Eva Blank, Rosanne Green, and Alison Benjamin. *Jokelopedia: The Biggest, Best, Silliest, Dumbest Joke Book Ever.* New York: Workman Publishing Company, 2006.

Internet Addresses

National Institute of Environmental Health Sciences Kids' Pages
<http://kids.niehs.nih.gov/rd1.htm>

Activity Village: Jokes for Kids!
<http://www.activityvillage.co.uk/kids_jokes.htm>

Index

A
astronauts, 10

B
balance, 43
banana, 23, 24
blood, 26, 30, 31
bones, 17–20
brain, 37–41

C
carrots, 6
cells, 23, 39
chewing, 26, 28

D
dentist, 25, 27, 28
doctor, 4, 6, 14, 29, 30, 37

E
ears, 42–45
Empire State Building, 34
eyes, 4–8

F
face, 35
fingers, 13–16
fish, 9, 38
forearm, 15

G
growling (stomach), 11

H
hands, 15
head, 6, 19, 37, 39, 40
hearing, 43
heart, 29–32

I
inner ear, 43
intestines, 11
iris, 5

L
limerick, 8
lion, 7, 27

M
milk, 18
monsters, 9, 10, 37
muscles, 15, 33–36

O
organs, 23, 31, 39

P
palm, 15
pupil, 5

R
rabbit, 6, 42

S
senses, 43
septum, 31
sheep, 6, 8

sight, 4, 43
skeleton, 18, 19, 20
skin, 21–24
sleep, 8, 20, 38
smell, 7, 43
snake, 14, 24
stomach, 9–12

T
taste, 43
teeth, 25–28
thighbone, 19
toes, 15, 19
tongue twister, 7
touch, 43

V
Valentine, 29
vampire, 10, 26

W
witches, 5